Look and See 3

ACTIVITY BOOK

Gregg Schroeder

NATIONAL GEOGRAPHIC LEARNING

Australia • Brazil • Mexico • Singapore • United Kingdom • United States

Back to School

1 TR: 0.1 Listen and match. Then say.

1 2 3 4

1 TR: 0.2 Listen and chant. Then say.

Monday	Tuesday	Wednesday	Thursday
1 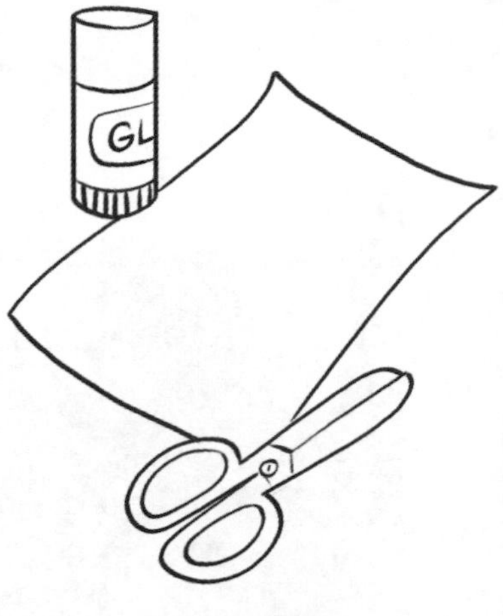	2 	3 	4 

Friday	Saturday	Sunday
5 	6 	7 

STRUCTURE: *What day is it today? It's Monday.*

UNIT

1 In Class

1 TR: 1.1 Listen. Circle ✔ or ✘.

1 ✔ ✘

2 ✔ ✘

3 ✔ ✘

4 ✔ ✘

5 ✔ ✘

6 ✔ ✘

7 ✔ ✘

2 Point and say.

NEW WORDS: *count to ten, draw a picture, make a craft, play a game, read a book, sing a song, write letters*

1 TR: 1.2 Listen and match. Then point and say.

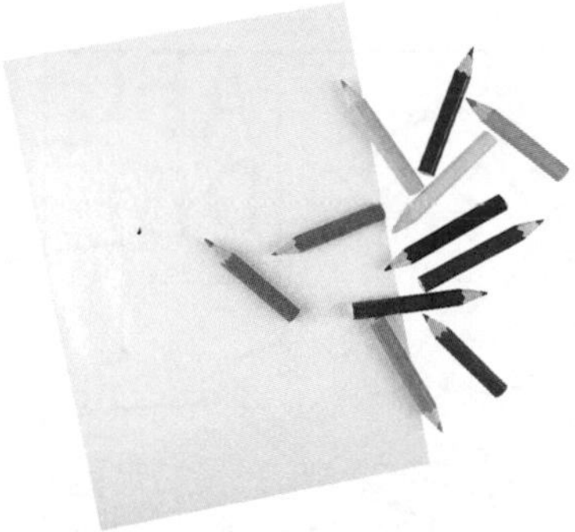

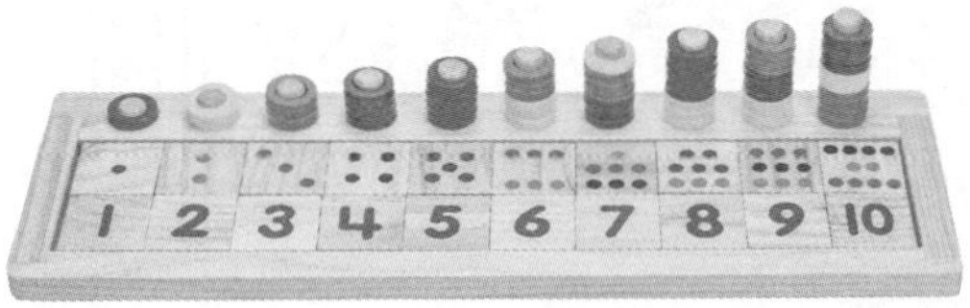

1 2 3 4 5 6 7

1 TR: 1.3 Find and say. Then listen and sing.

2 Write ✔ or ✘.

VALUE **Work hard at school.**

1 ☐

2 ☐

3 ☐

1 TR: 1.4 Listen and trace. Say.

1

cat

cat

2

rat

rat

2 Trace.

cat cat

cat cat

rat rat

rat rat

1 Match. Color and say.

9 + 1 = 10

3 + 1 = 4

5 + 1 = 6

 VIDEO: SC: 2 *(optional)* **Content Words:** *add, cupcake, more*

1 Say and color. Then play.

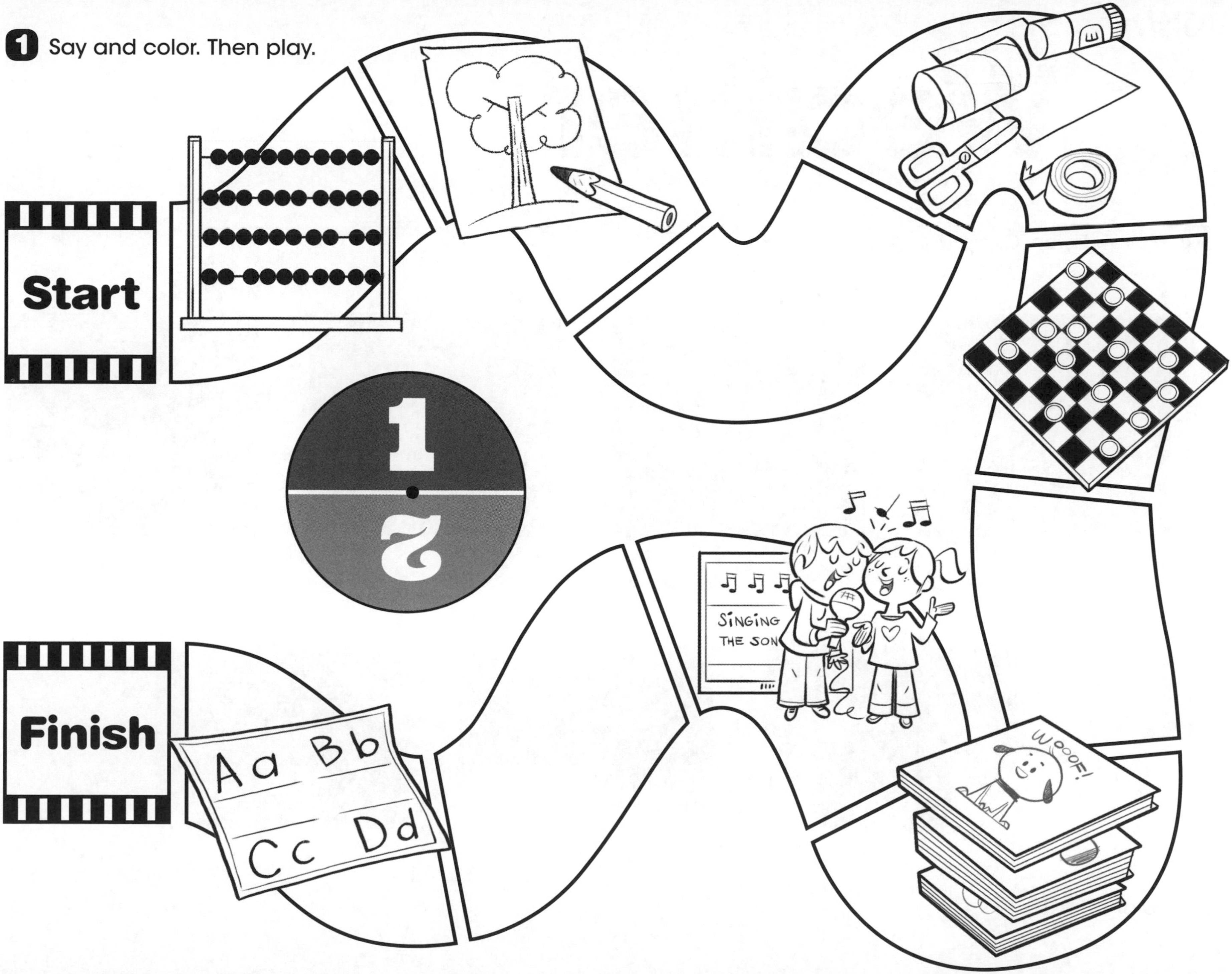

REVIEW: NEW WORDS: *count to ten, draw a picture, make a craft, play a game, read a book, sing a song, write letters*
STRUCTURE: *Let's draw a picture. OK, good idea!/No, thanks.*

UNIT

2 Weather

1 TR: 2.1 Listen. Circle ✔ or ✘.

1 ✔ ✘

2 ✔ ✘

3 ✔ ✘

4 ✔ ✘

5 ✔ ✘

6 ✔ ✘

7 ✔ ✘

2 Point and say.

NEW WORDS: *cloudy, cold, hot, rainy, snowy, sunny, windy*

1 TR: 2.2 Listen and match. Then point and say.

1 2 3 4 5 6 7

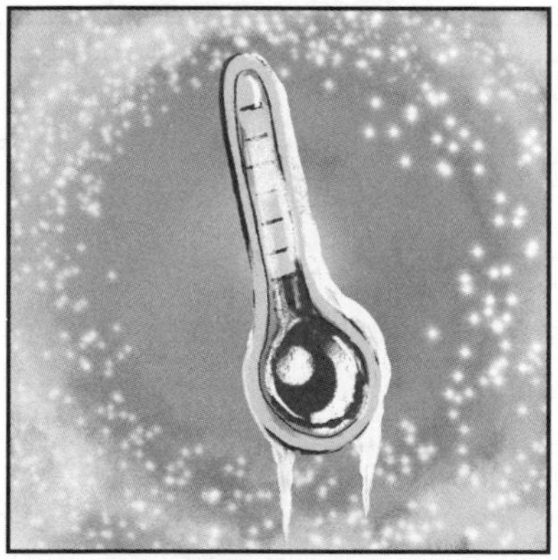

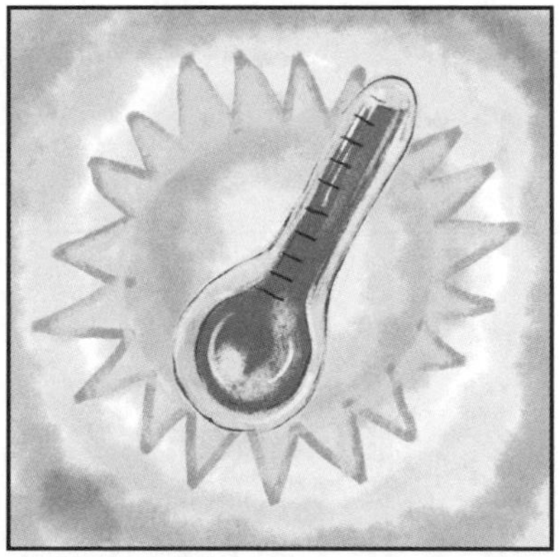

1 TR: 2.3 Point and say. Then sing. Color.

2 Write ✔ or ✘.

VALUE Be careful in the sun.

1 ☐

2 ☐

3 ☐

1 TR: 2.4 Listen and trace. Say.

1

man

man

2

van

van

2 Trace.

man man

man man

van van

van van

1 Point and say.

 VIDEO: SC: 4 *(optional)* **Content Words:** *cloud, down, rain, steam, up*

1 Color and say.

REVIEW: NEW WORDS: *cloudy, cold, hot, rainy, snowy, sunny, windy*
STRUCTURE: *What's the weather like? It's sunny.*

UNIT

3 My Community

1 TR: 3.1 Listen and match.

1 2 3 4 5 6 7 8

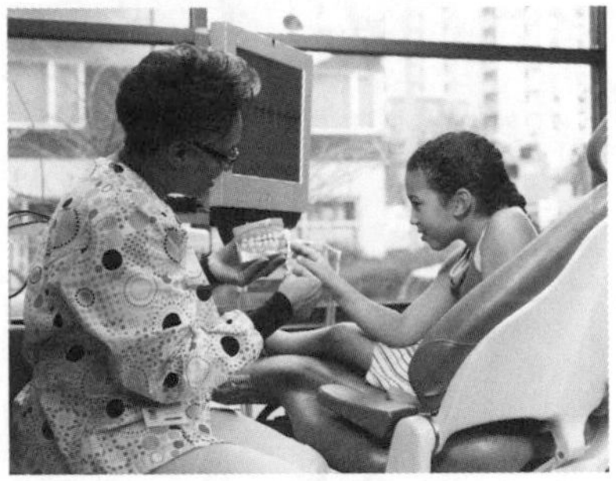

2 Point and say.

NEW WORDS: *bus driver, dentist, doctor, firefighter, librarian, mail carrier, police officer, vet*

1 TR: 3.2 Listen and point. Then say.

STRUCTURE: *Is he/she a doctor? Yes, he/she is./No, he/she isn't.*

1 TR: 3.3 Listen and color.

2 Write or .

VALUE **Be polite.**

1 ☐

2 ☐

3 ☐

1 TR: 3.4 Listen and trace. Say.

1 bed

bed

2 red

red

2 Trace.

b e d b e d

b e d b e d

r e d r e d

r e d r e d

1 TR: 3.5 Listen and point. Then say.

1

2

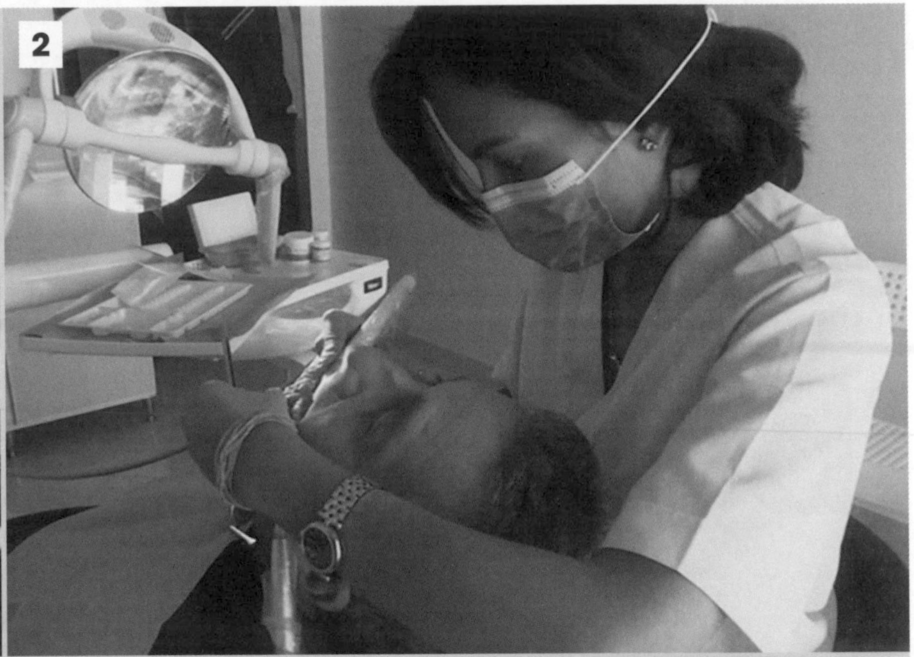

3

4

 VIDEO: SC: 6 *(optional)* **Content Words:** *help, people*

1 TR: 3.6 Listen and match. Then say.

1

2

3

4

5

6

7

8

REVIEW: NEW WORDS: *bus driver, dentist, doctor, firefighter, librarian, mail carrier, police officer, vet*
STRUCTURE: *Is he/she a doctor? Yes, he/she is./No, he/she isn't.*

UNIT 4

Make Some Noise!

1 TR: 4.1 Listen. Write ✔ or ✘.

1 ☑

2 ☐

3 ☐

4 ☐

5 ☐

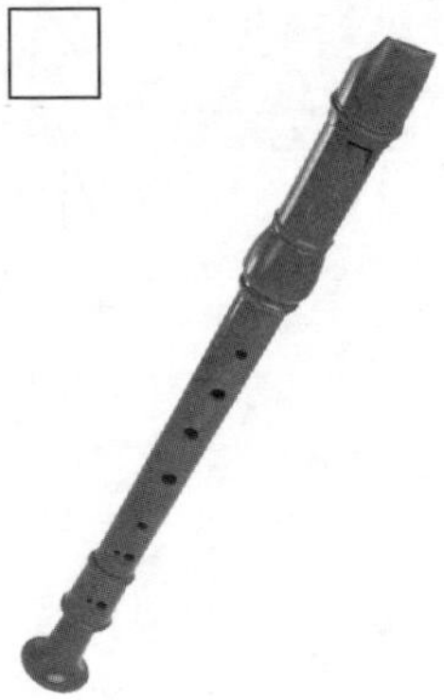

6 ☐

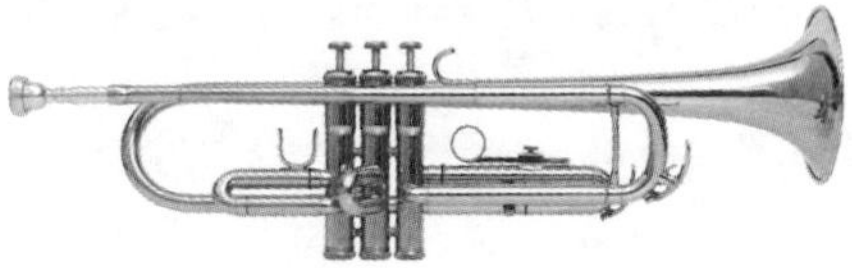

7 ☐

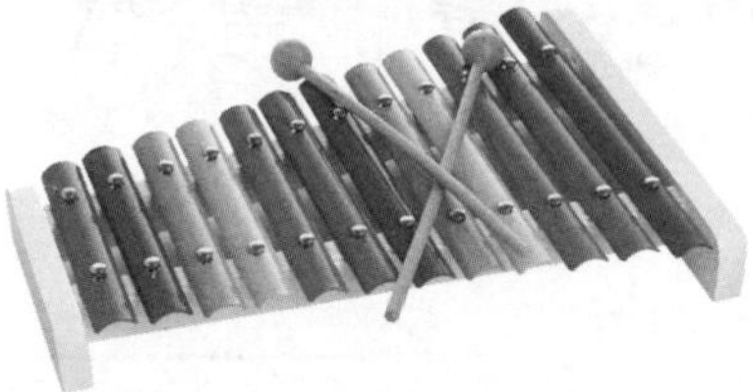

8 ☐

2 Point and say.

NEW WORDS: *drums, guitar, piano, recorder, tambourine, trumpet, violin, xylophone*

1 TR: 4.2 Listen and match. Then point and say.

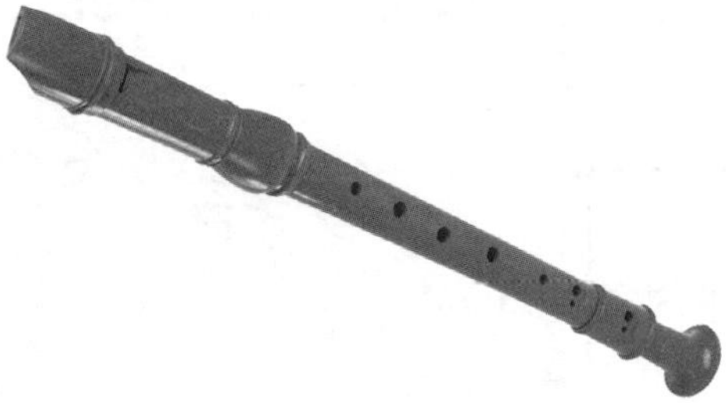

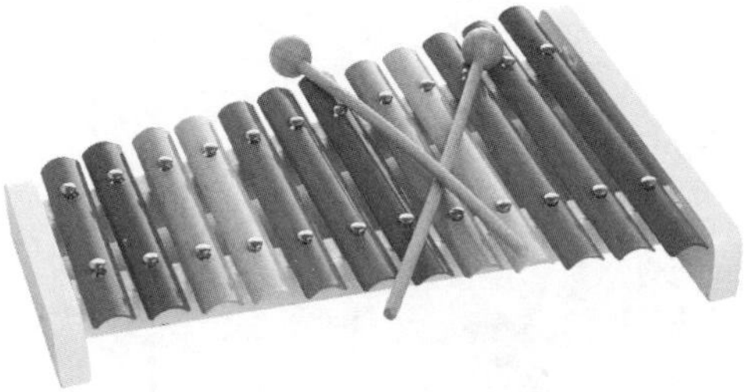

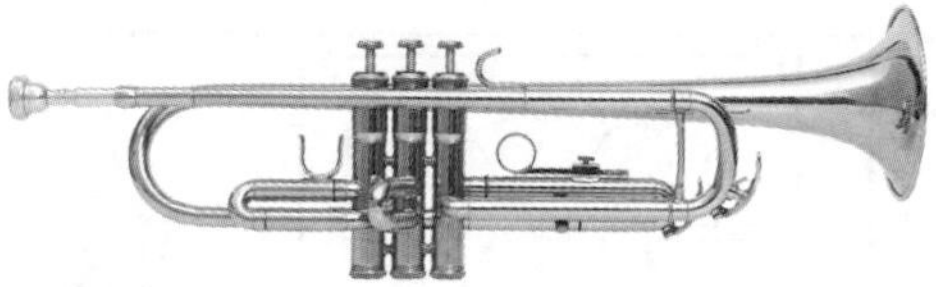

STRUCTURE: *He can play the piano. She can play the guitar.*

1 TR: 4.3 Listen and circle. Then sing and point.

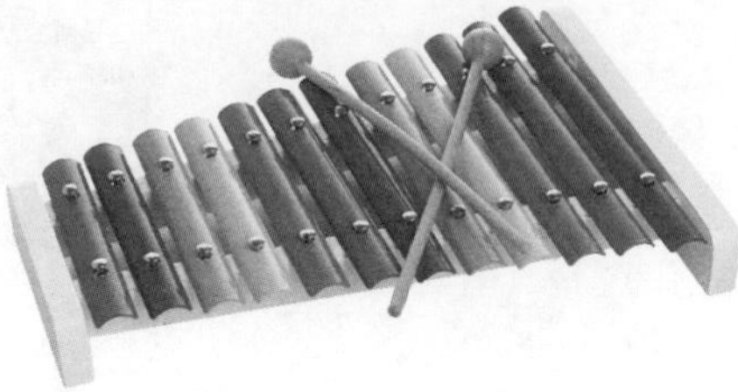

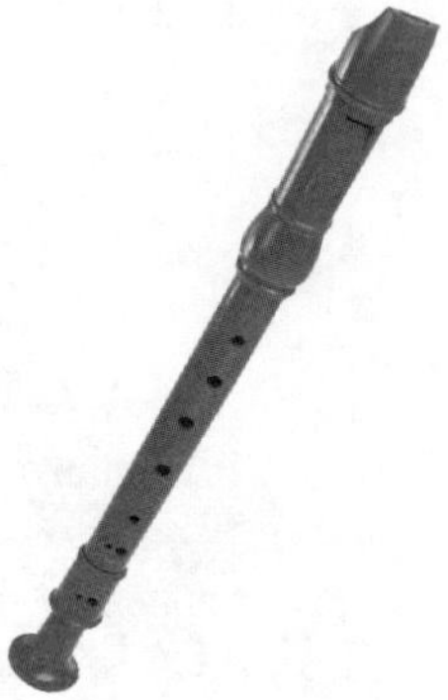

2 Write ✔ or ✘.

VALUE **Work together.**

1 ☐

2 ☐

3 ☐

1 TR: 4.4 Listen and trace. Say.

1

pet

pet

2

vet

vet

2 Trace.

pet pet

pet pet

vet vet

vet vet

1 Point and say. Then color.

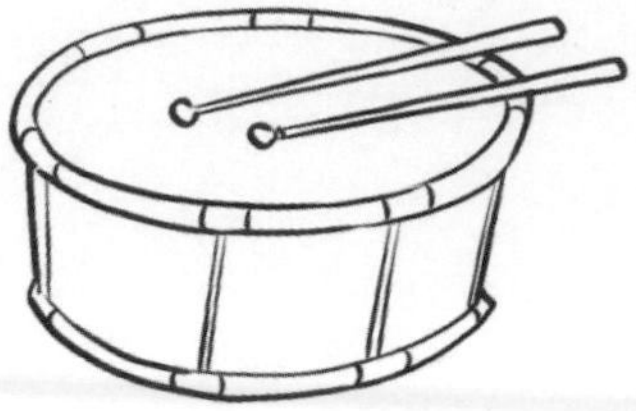

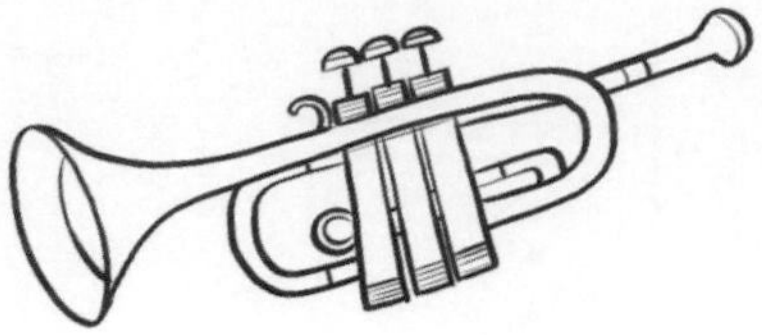

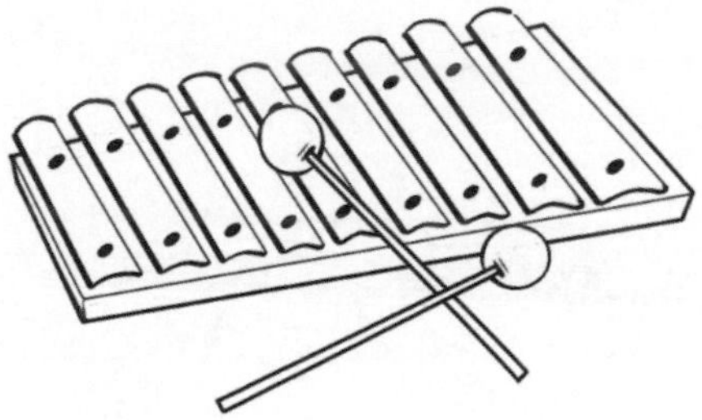

VIDEO: SC: 8 *(optional)* **Content Words:** *percussion, stringed, wind*

1 Say. Then play and do.

REVIEW: NEW WORDS: *drums, guitar, piano, recorder, tambourine, trumpet, violin, xylophone*
STRUCTURE: *He can play the piano. She can play the guitar.*

UNIT

5 Shapes Around Us

1 TR: 5.1 Listen and match.

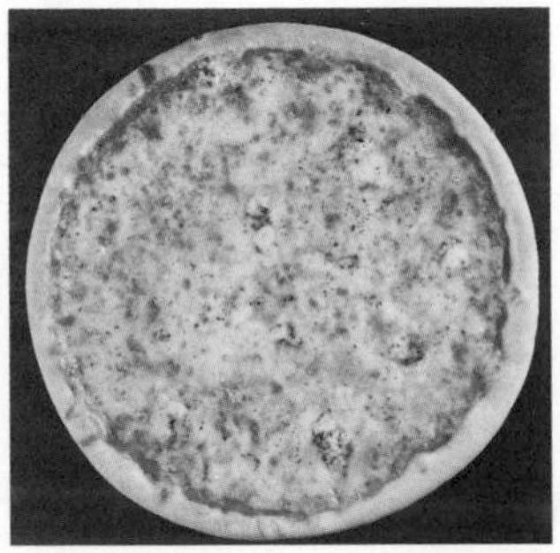

1 2 3 4 5 6 7 8

2 Point and say.

 NEW WORDS: *circle, diamond, hexagon, oval, rectangle, square, star, triangle*

1 TR: 5.2 Listen and color. Then count and say.

1 TR: 5.3 Listen and color. Then sing.

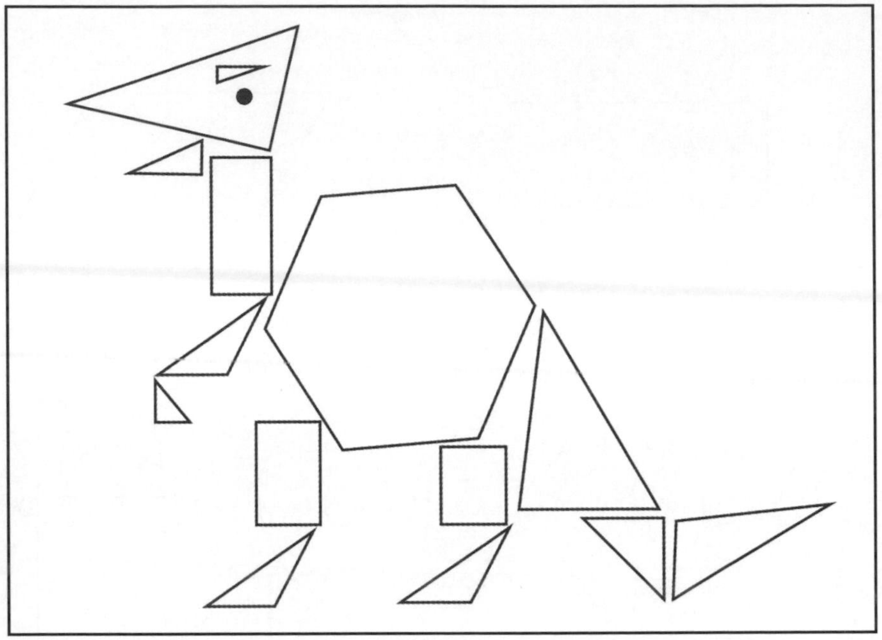

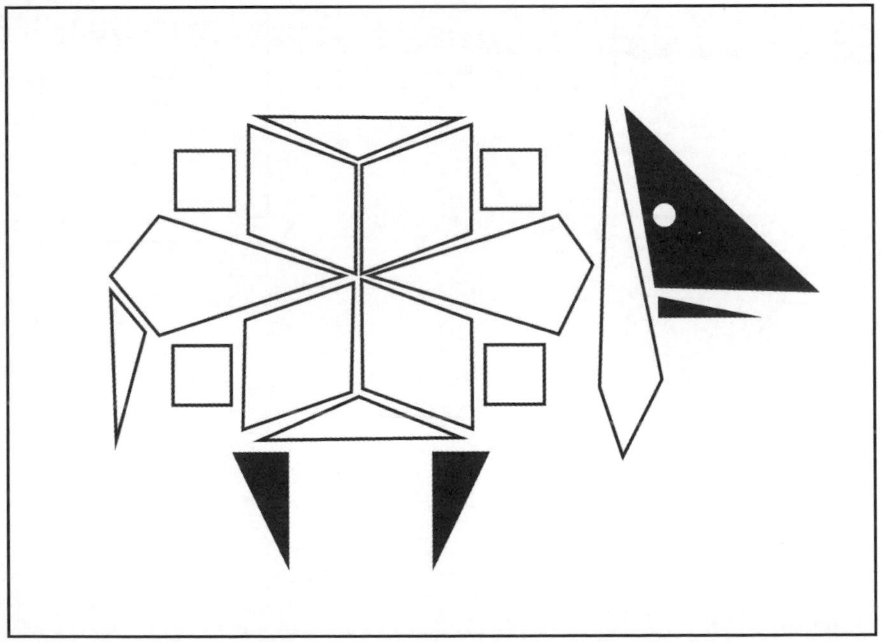

2 Write ✔ or ✘.

VALUE Use your imagination.

1 ☐

2 ☐

3 ☐

1 TR: 5.4 Listen and trace. Say.

1 mix

mix

2 six

six

2 Trace.

mix mix

mix mix

six six

six six

1 TR: 5.5 Listen and match. Then say.

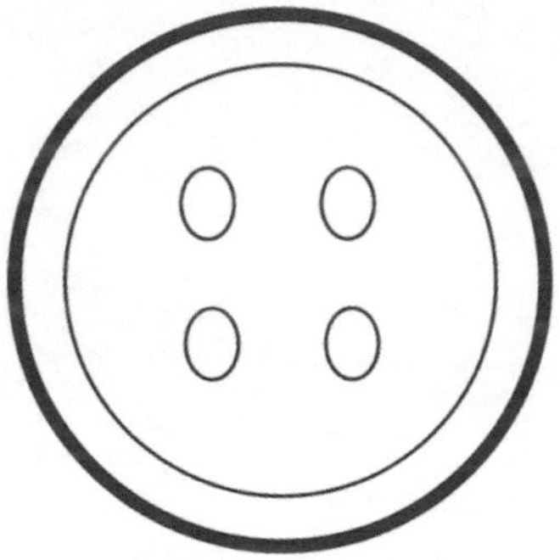

 VIDEO: SC: 10 *(optional)* **Content Words:** *cube, flat, pyramid, sphere, world*

1 Say and color. Then play.

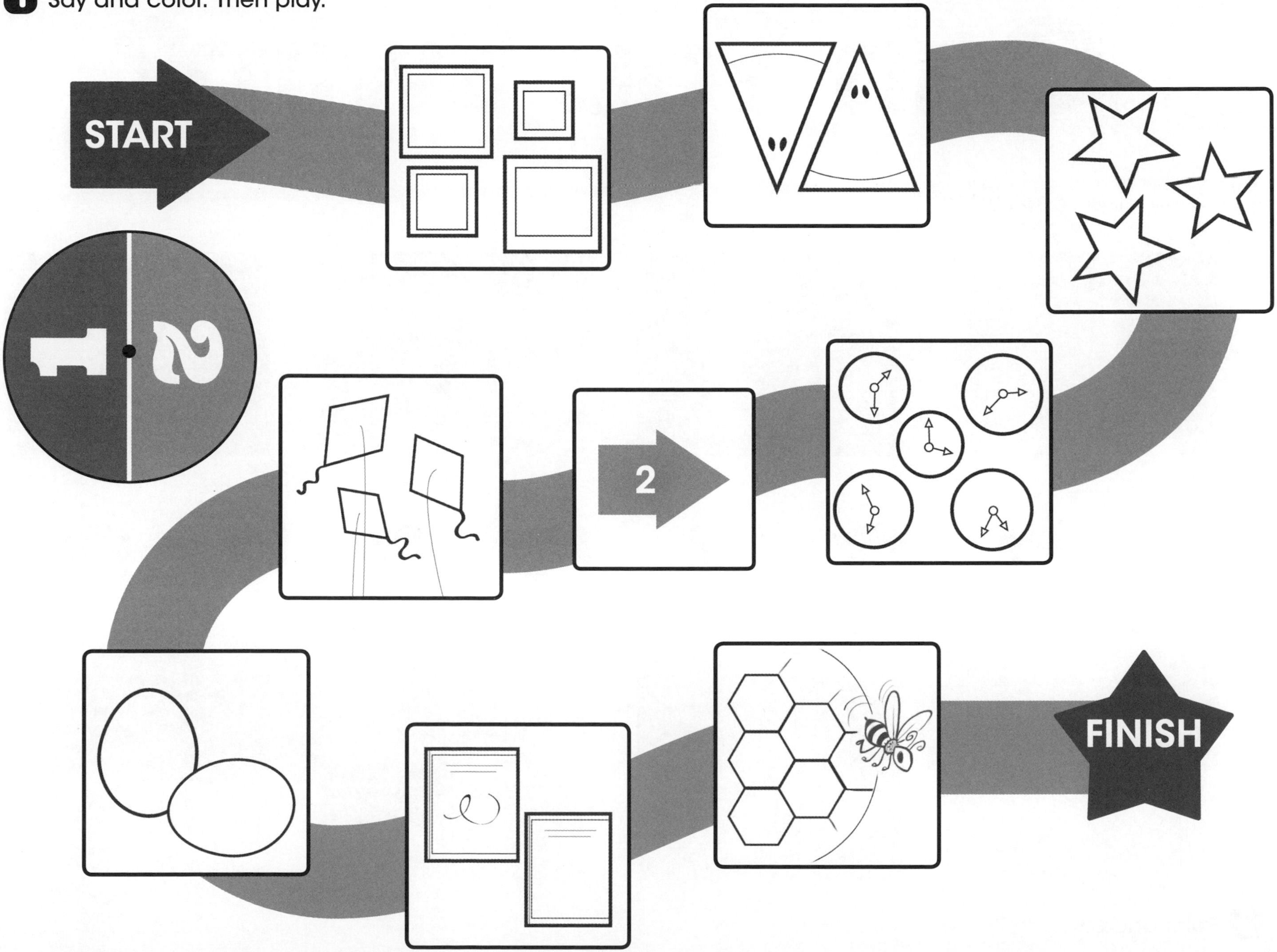

UNIT

6 Can You Swim?

1 TR: 6.1 Listen and match.

1 2 3 4 5 6 7 8

2 Point and say.

 NEW WORDS: *catch, climb, fly, kick, ride, skip, swim, throw*

1 TR: 6.2 Listen and circle. Then say.

STRUCTURE: *Can you skip? Yes, I can./No, I can't.*

1 TR: 6.3 Listen and color.

2 Write ✔ or ✘.

VALUE Try again.

1 ☐

2 ☐

3 ☐

1 TR: 6.4 Listen and trace. Say.

1 big

big

2 dig

dig

2 Trace.

big big

big big

dig dig

dig dig

1 TR: 6.5 Listen and match. Then say.

1

2

3

 VIDEO: SC: 12 *(optional)* **Content Word:** *penguin*

1 Say and color. Then play.

REVIEW: NEW WORDS: *catch, climb, fly, kick, ride, skip, swim, throw*
STRUCTURE: *Can you skip? Yes, I can./No, I can't.*

UNIT

7 At Home

1 TR: 7.1 Listen and circle ✔ or ✘.

1 ✔ ✘

2 ✔ ✘

3 ✔ ✘

4 ✔ ✘

5 ✔ ✘

6 ✔ ✘

7 ✔ ✘

8 ✔ ✘

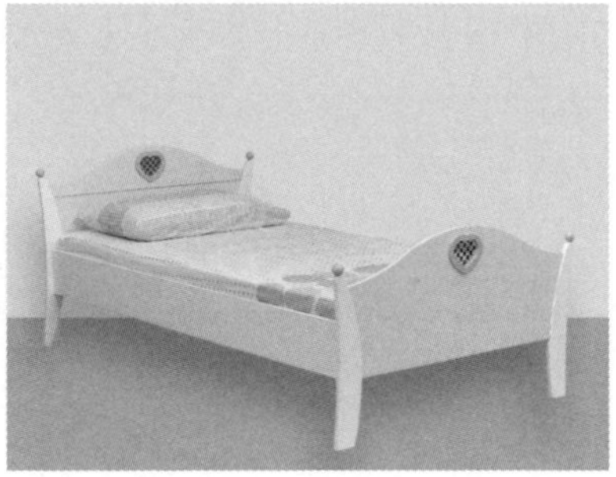

2 Point and say.

NEW WORDS: *bathroom, bedroom, kitchen, living room; bed, shelf, sink, sofa; welcome*

1 TR: 7.2 Listen and match.

1 2 3 4 5 6

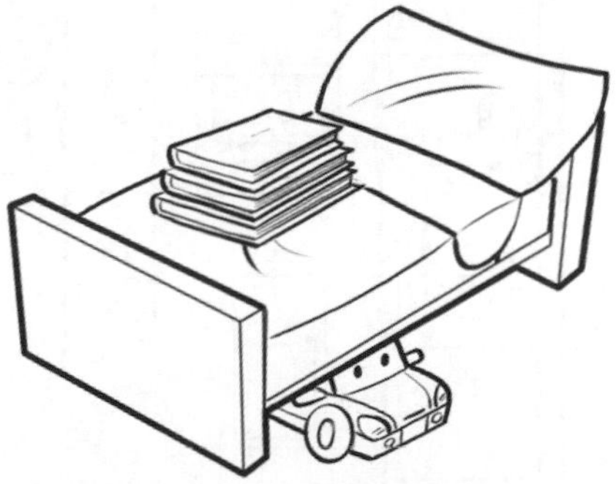

1 TR: 7.3 Listen and find. Then sing.

2 Write ✔ or ✘.

VALUE **Help at home.**

1 ☐

2 ☐

3 ☐

1 TR: 7.4 Listen and trace. Say.

1

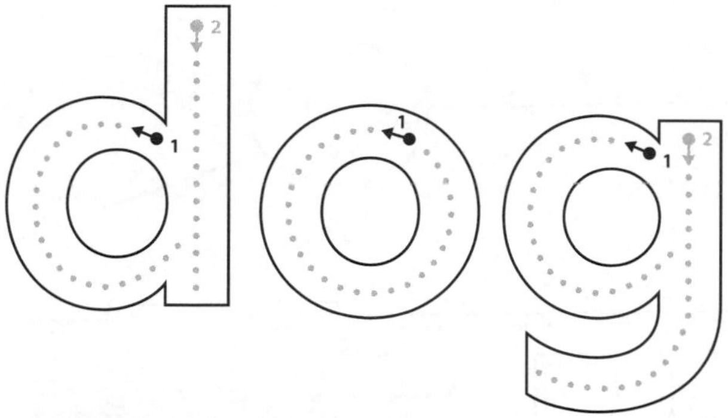

dog

2

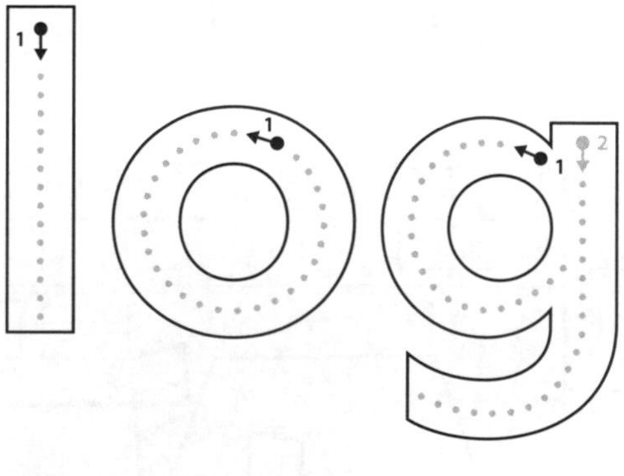

log

2 Trace.

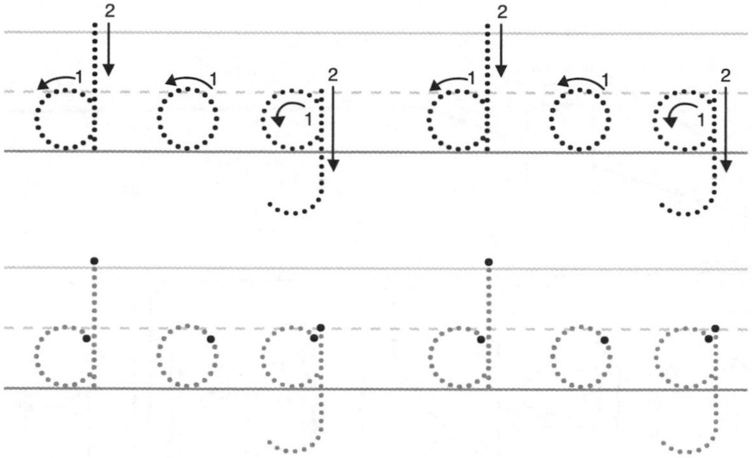

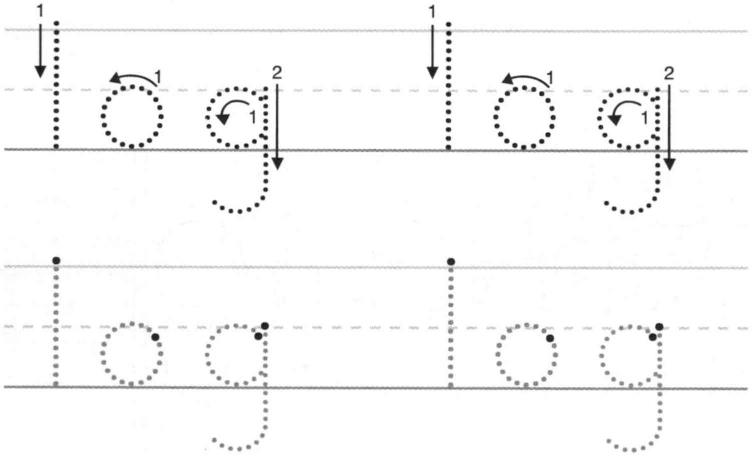

1 TR: 7.5 Listen and point.

VIDEO: SC: 14 *(optional)* **Content Words:** *apartment, city, country, garden, house*

1 Draw and say.

REVIEW: NEW WORDS: *bedroom, bathroom, kitchen, living room; bed, shelf, sink, sofa; welcome*
STRUCTURE: *The picture is in the bathroom. The cars are under the bed.*

UNIT

8 My Special Place

1 TR: 8.1 Listen. Write ✔ or ✘.

1 ☐

2 ☐

3 ☐

4 ☐

5 ☐

6 ☐

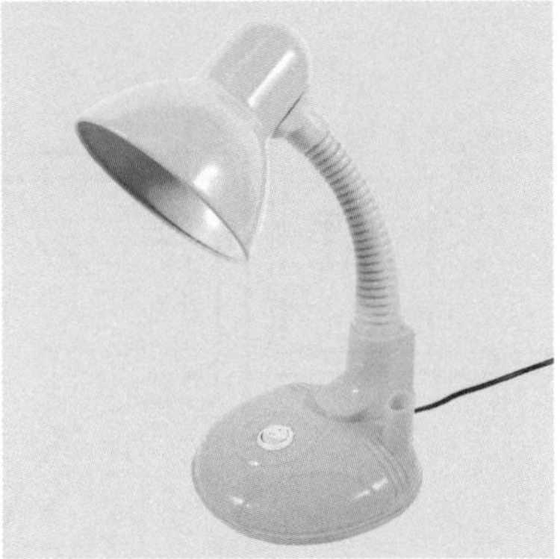

7 ☐

8 ☐

2 Point and say.

NEW WORDS: *blanket, door, lamp, pillow, rug, toy box, tree house, window*

1 What's different? Say.

1

2

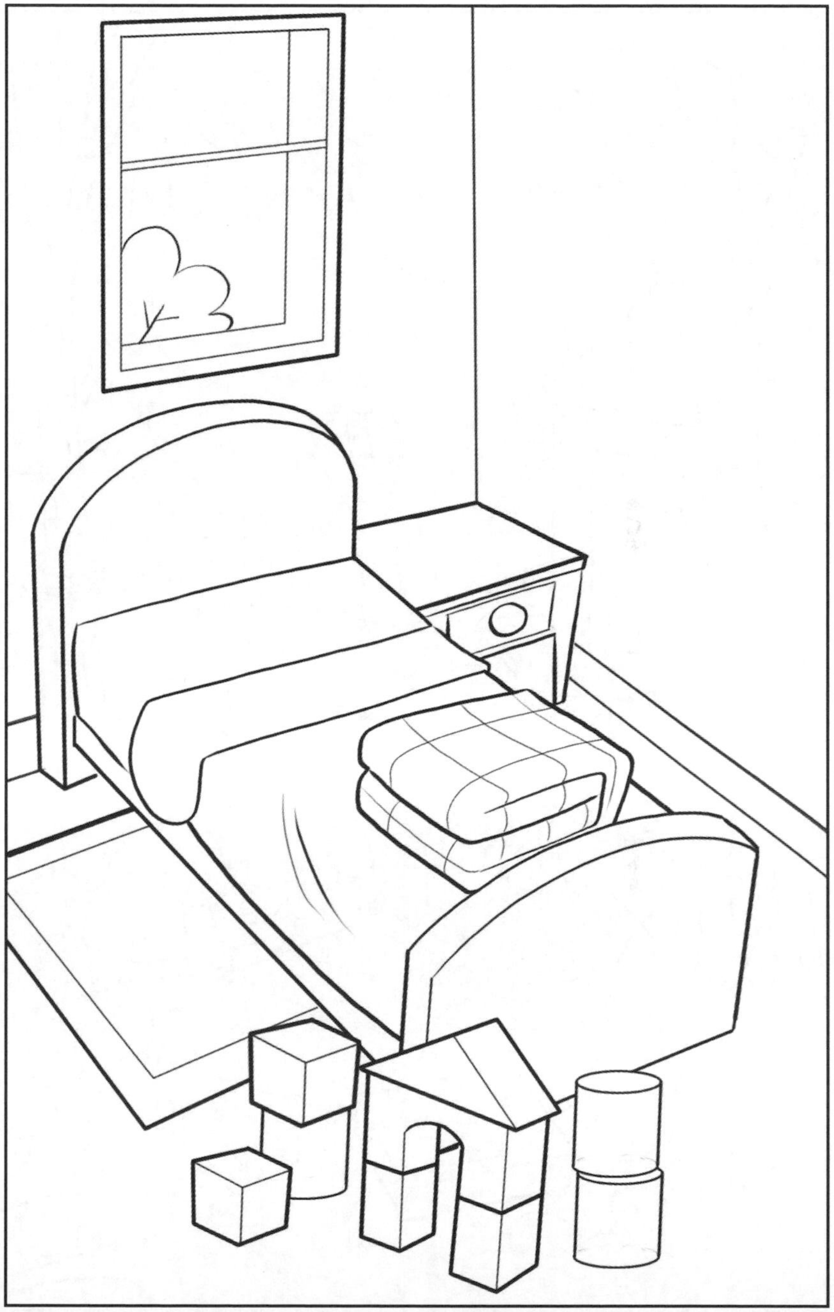

STRUCTURE: *Is there a rug? Yes, there is./No, there isn't.*

1 TR: 8.2 Listen and color.

2 Write ✔ or ✘.

VALUE Be welcoming.

1 ☐

2 ☐

3 ☐

1 TR: 8.3 Listen and trace. Say.

1 box

box

2 fox

fox

2 Trace.

box box

box box

fox fox

fox fox

1 TR: 8.4 Listen and match.

1

2

3

 VIDEO: SC: 16 *(optional)* **Content Words:** *hole, nest, squirrel*

1 Color and say.

REVIEW: NEW WORDS: *blanket, door, lamp, pillow, rug, toy box, tree house, window*
STRUCTURE: *Is there a rug? Yes, there is./No, there isn't.*

UNIT

9 Under the Sea

1 TR: 9.1 Listen and match.

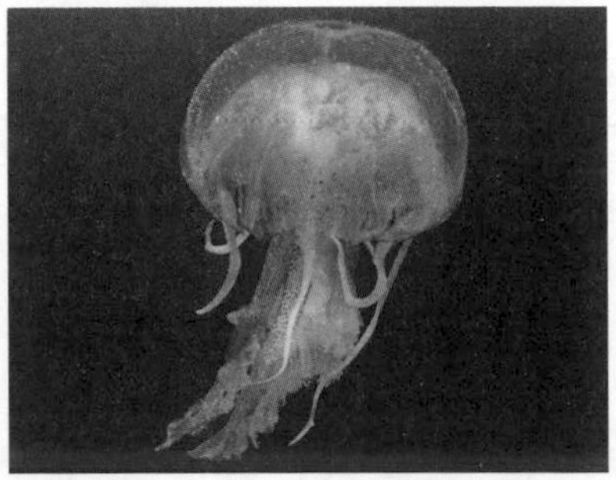

1 2 3 4 5 6 7 8

2 Point and say.

 NEW WORDS: *crab, dolphin, jellyfish, octopus, seahorse, shark, starfish, turtle*

1 Play and say.

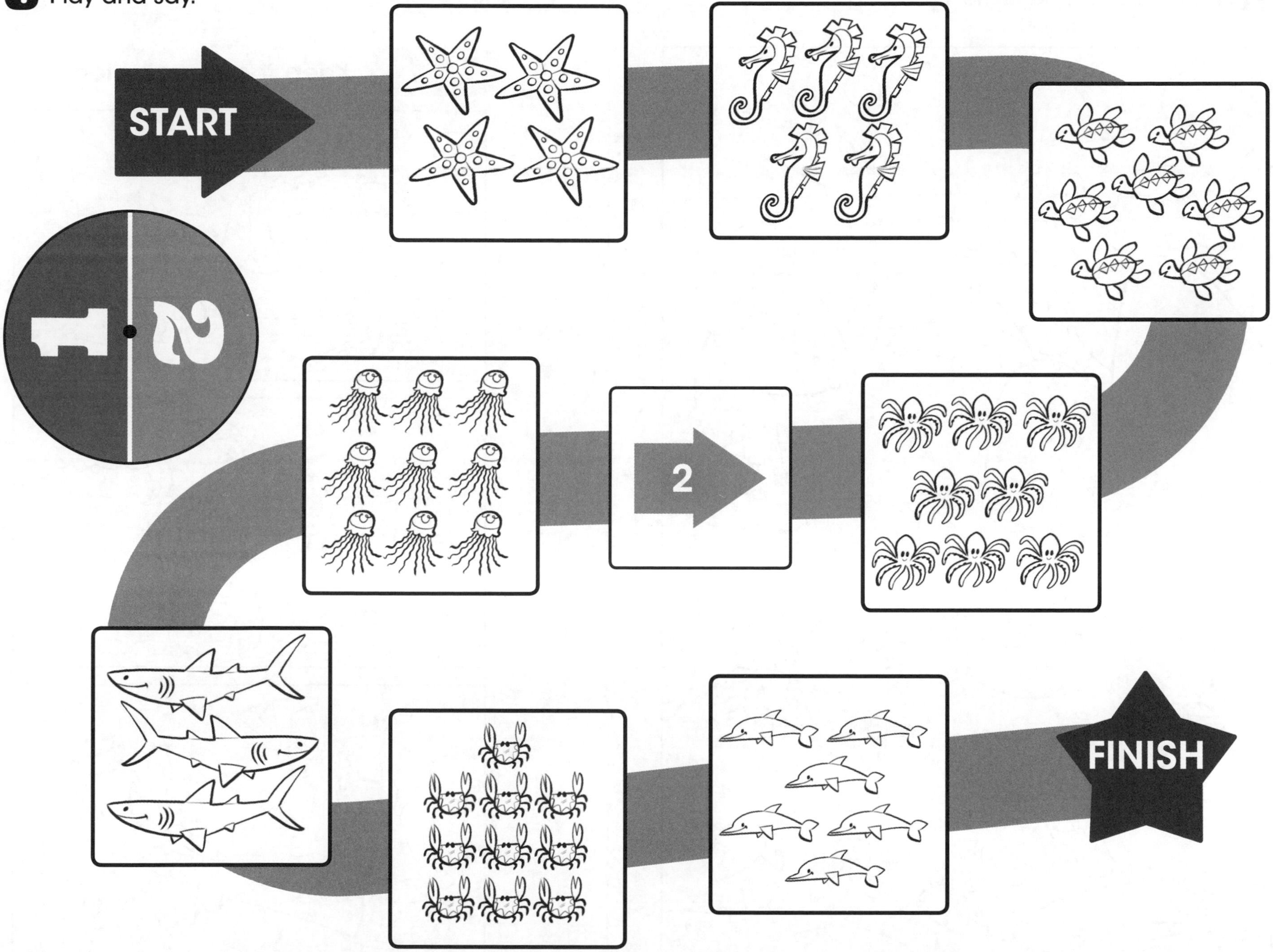

STRUCTURE: *How many crabs are there? There are fourteen crabs.*

1 TR: 9.2 Listen and circle. Then sing.

2 Write ✔ or ✘.

VALUE **Keep the beach clean.**

1 ☐

2 ☐

3 ☐

1 TR: 9.3 Listen and trace. Say.

1

run

run

2

sun

sun

2 Trace.

run run

run run

sun sun

sun sun

1 TR: 9.4 Listen and point. Then color.

1 Count and say. Then play.

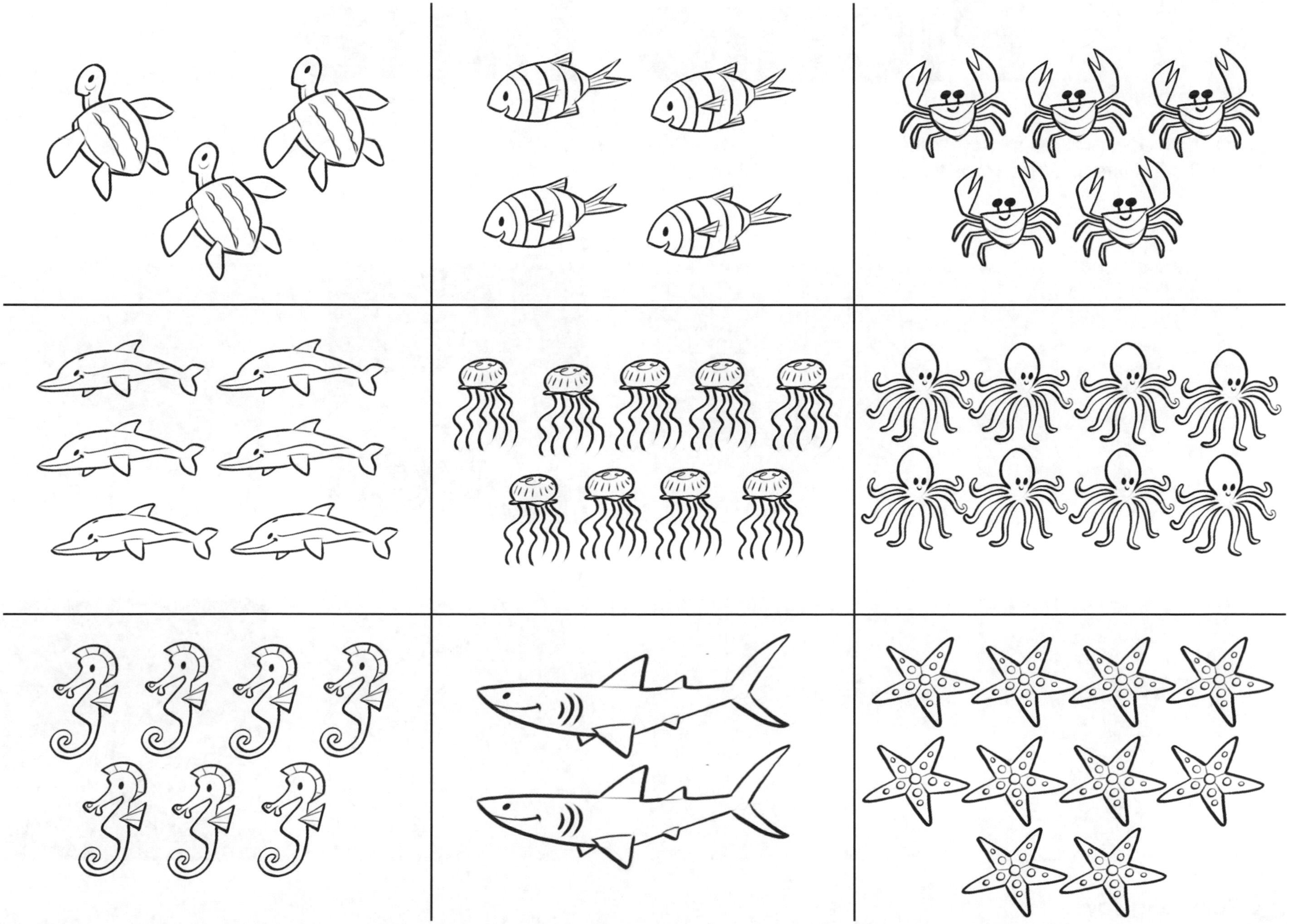

REVIEW: NEW WORDS: *crab, dolphin, jellyfish, octopus, seahorse, shark, starfish, turtle*
STRUCTURE: *How many crabs are there? There are fourteen crabs.*

UNIT 10 Picnic Time

1 TR: 10.1 Listen. Write ✔ or ✘.

1 ☐

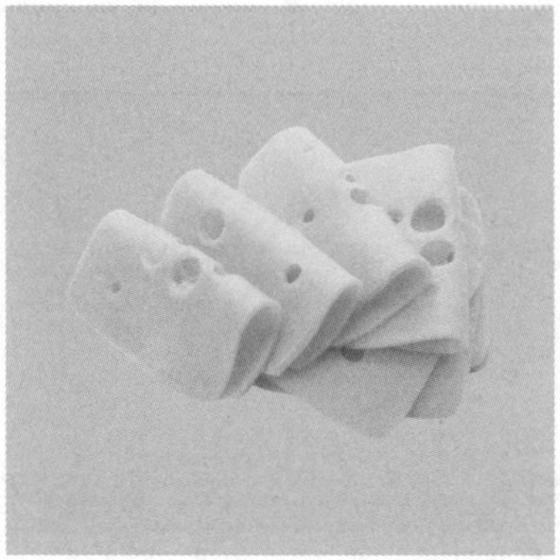

2 ☐

3 ☐

4 ☐

5 ☐

6 ☐

7 ☐

8 ☐

2 Point and say.

NEW WORDS: *cheese, fruit, juice, lemonade, sandwich, picnic, vegetables, yogurt*

1 TR: 10.2 Listen and circle. Then say.

1

2

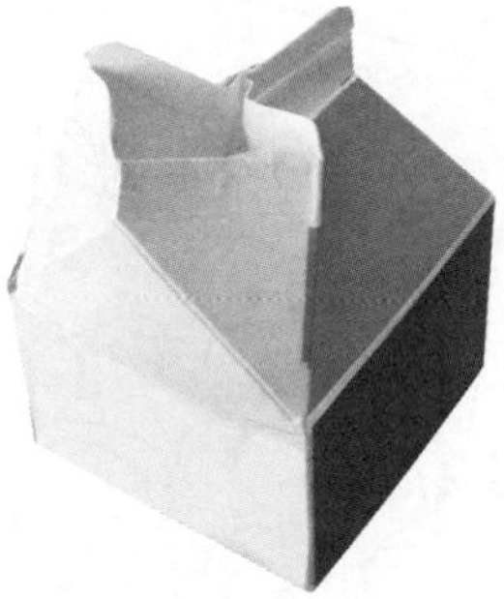

3

4

5

6

STRUCTURE: *Do you like fruit? Yes, I do./No, I don't.*

1 TR: 10.3 Listen and color.

2 Write ✔ or ✘.

VALUE Try new things.

1 ☐

2 ☐

3 ☐

1 TR: 10.4 Listen and trace. Say.

1

bug

2

mug

2 Trace.

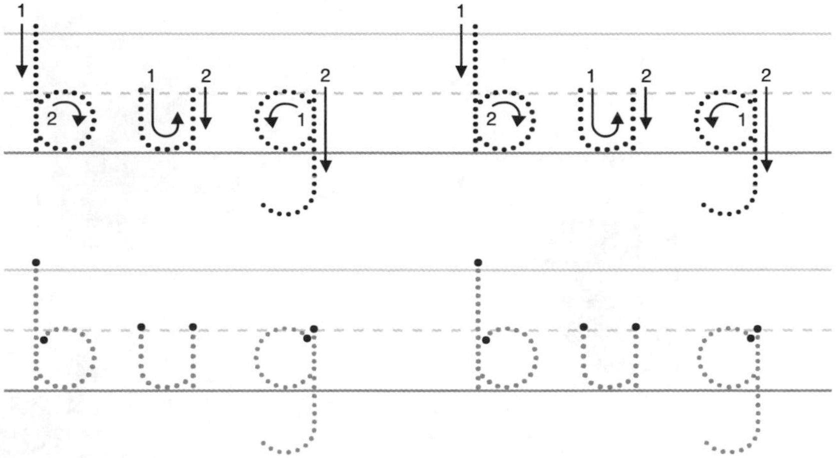

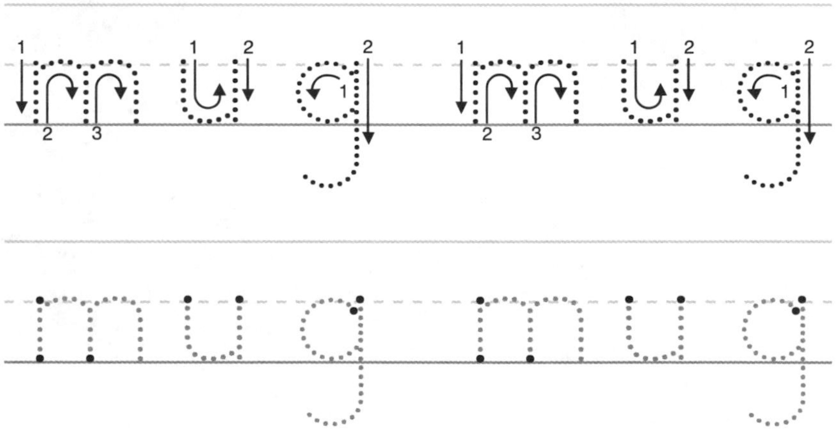

1 TR: 10.5 Match. Then listen and check.

 VIDEO: SC: 20 *(optional)* **Content Words:** *dairy, grain, healthy, protein*

1 Color. Draw and say.

REVIEW: NEW WORDS: *cheese, fruit, juice, lemonade, picnic, sandwich, vegetables, yogurt*
STRUCTURE: *Do you like fruit? Yes, I do./No, I don't.*

CREDITS

PHOTOS: 4 (tl) Cultura RM Exclusive/Hybrid Images/Getty Images; (tml) RayArt Graphics/Alamy Stock Photo; (tmr) Klaus Vedfelt/DigitalVision/Getty Images; (tr) Bjarte Rettedal/DigitalVision/Getty Images; (bl) Kurt Hoerbst/Anzenberger/Redux; (bm) David Jakle/Image Source/Getty Images; (br) Nadezhda1906/iStock/Getty Images; **5** (tl) Emilija Randjelovic/iStock/Getty Images; (tml) Derek Hatfield/Shutterstock.com; (tmr) Pingun/Shutterstock.com; (tr) agil73/Shutterstock.com; (bl) Eye Ubiquitous/Alamy Stock Photo; (bm) Africa Studio/Shutterstock.com; (br) Kurt Hoerbst/Anzenberger/Redux; **10** (tl) Tang Ming Tung/DigitalVision/Getty Images; (tml, tmr) Jessica Moore/Cultura/Getty Images; (tr) Secheltgirl/Shutterstock.com; (bl) Onjira Leibe/Shutterstock.com; (bm) Glasshouse Images/Alamy Stock Photo; (br) © Andrew Suryono; **16** (tl) kali9/E+/Getty Images; (tml) Hill Street Studios/DigitalVision/Getty Images; (tmr) JHMimagine/iStock Editorial/Getty Images; (tr) Johan Ordonez/AFP/Getty Images; (bl) Thomas Barwick/DigitalVision/Getty Images; (bml) Hero Images/Getty Images; (bmr) Yu Fangping Xinhua/eyevine/Redux; (br) Johannes Eisele/AFP/Getty Images; **20** (tl) GeorgiaCourt/Creatas Video/Getty Images; (tr) AP Archive; (bl) shironosov/Creatas Video+/Getty Images; (br) AP Archive; **22** (tl) Creative Crop/Photodisc/Getty Images; (tml) Boris Medvedev/Shutterstock.com; (tmr) Africa Studio/Shutterstock.com; (tr) AlexMaster/iStock/Getty Images; (bl) Emin Ozkan/Shutterstock.com; (bml) Walter Bilotta/Shutterstock.com; (bmr) Dave King (c) Dorling Kindersley/Dorling Kindersley/Getty Images; (br) ArtyuStudio/Shutterstock.com; **23** (tl) Emin Ozkan/Shutterstock.com; (tr) Boris Medvedev/Shutterstock.com; (ml) Walter Bilotta/Shutterstock.com; (mr) Dave King (c) Dorling Kindersley/Dorling Kindersley/Getty Images; (bl) Africa Studio/Shutterstock.com; (br) AlexMaster/iStock/Getty Images; **24** (tl) Creative Crop/Photodisc/Getty Images; (tr) Dave King (c) Dorling Kindersley/Dorling Kindersley/Getty Images; (ml) AlexMaster/iStock/Getty Images; (cr) Emin Ozkan/Shutterstock.com; (bl) Africa Studio/Shutterstock.com; (br) Boris Medvedev/Shutterstock.com; **28** (tl) Maksim Denisenko/Shutterstock.com; (tml) Gavin Zeigler/Alamy Stock Photo; (tmr) Ann Yuni/Shutterstock.com; (tr) J-Roman/E+/Getty Images; (bl) Gerard Lacz/Minden Pictures; (bml) Matteo Colombo/moment/Getty Images; (bmr) © Holly Awward; (br) Madeleine Fitzsimons/Alamy Stock Photo; **32** (tl) James P. Blair/National Geographic Image Collection; (tm) Jay's photo/moment/Getty Images; (tr) Steve and Donna O'Meara/National Geographic Image Collection; (bl) Ivan Kmit/Alamy Stock Photo; (bm) Picsfive/Shutterstock.com; (br) The World in HDR/Shutterstock.com; **34** (tl) Dev Carr/Cultura/Getty Images; (tml) Joel Sartore/National Geographic Image Collection; (tmr) Shanna Szymczak/EyeEm/Getty Images; (tr) Donald Iain Smith/Moment/Getty Images; (bl) Carolyn Jenkins/Alamy Stock Photo; (bml) David Madison/Photographer's Choice/Getty Images; (bmr) Olivier Renck/Aurora Open/Getty Images; (br) © Seth Casteel; **35** (tl) Camille Tokerud/The Image Bank/Getty Images; (tm) Viacheslav Iakobchuk/Alamy Stock Photo; (tr) Ariel Skelley/DigitalVision/Getty Images; (ml) selimaksan/E+/Getty Images; (mr) chuchiko17/Shutterstock.com; (bl) Thai Yuan Lim/EyeEm/Getty Images; (bml) Paul Blackley/Moment/Getty Images; (bmr) Johnnie Pakington/DigitalVision/Getty Images; (br) Juampiter/Moment/Getty Images; **38** (l) Michael Nichols/National Geographic Image Collection; (m) Jan Vermeer/Minden Pictures; (r) Design Pics Inc/National Geographic Image Collection; **40** (tl) Look Photography/UpperCut Images/Getty Images; (tml) Chris Clor/Tetra images/Getty Images; (tmr, bl) Helmut Hassenrueck/Picture Press/Redux; (tr, bml) John Keeble/Moment/Getty Images; (bmr) John Wollwerth/Shutterstock.com; (br) Venus Angel/Shutterstock.com; **46** (tl, tml) © The Master Wishmaker England; (tmr) New Africa/Shutterstock.com; (tr) Africa Studio/Shutterstock.com; (bl) Andy Crawford/Dorling Kindersley/Getty Images; (bml) phanasitti/iStock/Getty Images; (bmr) Zodiaccc/Shutterstock.com; (br) TissaNsk/Shutterstock.com; **50** (tl) B Christopher/Alamy Stock Photo; (tm) Maxine Bolton/EyeEm/Getty Images; (tr) Yaorusheng/Moment/Getty Images; (bl) Skip Moody/Alamy Stock Photo; (bm) Gunashekar S/500px/Getty Images; (br) Lorraine Bennery/Minden Pictures; **52** (tl) Otto Plantema/Minden Pictures; (tml) Kagii Yasuaki/Minden Pictures; (tmr) yfhishinuma/iStock/Getty Images; (tr) Scotland: The Big Picture/Minden Pictures; (bl) Seaphotoart/Shutterstock.com; (bml) Jane Burton/Nature Picture Library; (bmr) TheSP4N1SH/iStock/Getty Images; (br) Jurgen and Christine Sohns/Minden Pictures; **58** (tl) Africa Studio/Shutterstock.com; (tml) Elena Elisseeva/Shutterstock.com; (tmr, br) Malcolm P Chapman/Moment/Getty Images; (tr) Design Pics Inc/National Geographic Image Collection; (bl) MaraZe/Shutterstock.com; (bml) Hortimages/Shutterstock.com; (bmr) gowithstock/Shutterstock.com; **59** (tl) gowithstock/Shutterstock.com; (tml) Arina_Bogachyova/iStock/Getty Images; (tmr) Lukas Gojda/Shutterstock.com; (tr) Suzanne Tucker/Shutterstock.com; (ml) MaraZe/Shutterstock.com; (mml) Prostock-studio/Shutterstock.com; (mmr) bitt24/Shutterstock.com; (mr) New Africa/Shutterstock.com; (bl) Diana Taliun/Shutterstock.com; (bml) Creativeye99/iStock/Getty Images; (bmr) MaraZe/Shutterstock.com; (br) Rafa Elias/Moment/Getty Images; **62** (tl) Design Pics Inc/National Geographic Image Collection; (tml) Anton Starikov/Alamy Stock Photo; (tmr) Liudmyla Lysenko/Alamy Stock Photo; (tr) Judith Haeusler/Cultura/Getty Images; (ml) Nattawut Lakjit/EyeEm/Getty Images; (mml) YinYang/E+/Getty Images; (mmr) Olga Sapegina/Shutterstock.com; (mr) Suzanne Tucker/Shutterstock.com; (bl) pjohnson1/E+/Getty Images; (bml) Kovaleva_Ka/Shutterstock.com; (bmr) Marcelo De La Torre/EyeEm/Getty Images; (br) Iuliia Kochenkova/Shutterstock.com; **Back Cover** Joel Sartore/National Geographic Image Collection.

ILLUSTRATIONS: 2, 3, 6, 8, 9, 11, 12, 14, 15, 17, 18, 21, 24, 26, 27, 30, 32, 33, 36, 38, 39, 41, 42, 44, 45, 47, 48, 51, 53, 54, 56, 57, 60, 63 Giovanni Giorgi Pierfranceschi; **23, 35** Fabiana Faiallo.